A GUIDE TO

European Union Law and Institutions

Richard Wallis

Emerald Guides
www.emeraldpublishing.co.uk

Straightforward Publishing
Brighton BN2 4EG

British Cataloguing in Publication data. A catalogue record is
available for this book from the British Library.

ISBN 1847160 441
ISBN 13 9781847160447

Printed in the United Kingdom by Biddles Ltd Kings Lynn Norfolk

Cover Design by Bookworks Islington

Contents

Table of cases

Table of cases (alphabetical order)   p

Chapter 1

The Development of the European Union from 1945-57

European integration in the postwar period was shaped by two key developments. The first was the emergence of the cold war division of Europe. This had its roots in the Yalta summit of 1945, which divided Europe into 'spheres of influence'. Whilst the Western allies viewed the division as a temporary affair it very quickly became clear that the Soviet Union viewed it as permanent. Governments favourable to the interests of the then USSR were installed, leading Churchill to remark in his 1946 speech at Fulton, Missouri, that 'an iron curtain has descended across the European continent'.

In 1946, Churchill also spoke of the need to build a United States of Europe around a Franco-German axis to provide a structure to promote peace and stability.

The second key factor concerned the need to tackle the dire economic situation that affected European nations as a result of war having inflicted massive damage to countries infrastructure, housing, factories and roads. This difficult situation also impacted on Europe's ability to defend itself.

The Americans, under President Harry Truman pledged America's support. This was known as the 'Truman Doctrine' which was of immediate benefit to Europe.

The Marshall Plan

In June 1947, the Secretary of State General George Marshall outlined a plan, known widely as 'The Marshall Plan' to offer economic assistance to aid the recovery of all European states, declaring that ' Europe's requirements for the next three or for years of foreign food and all other essential products-principally from America-are so much greater than her present ability to pay that she must have substantial additional help or face economic, social and political deterioration of a very grave character'. The plan aimed to promote inter-European trade and create a marketplace that was similar to the US. In aiming to speed up the process of European recovery, the United States hoped that an upturn in Europe's fortunes would lessen the dependence on American aid.

Superpower influence in the European arena was reflected in the rapid assertion of Soviet influence in Eastern Europe. By 1948, Czechoslovakia, East Germany and Poland were under Soviet influence and in 1961, following a period of restricting access to Berlin by the Soviets, (which was lifted in 1949), followed by a period of airlifting of supplies to West Berlin by the Allies, the

Berlin wall was erected. The 'Berlin crisis' helped to institutionalise the cold war and influenced the decision of Britain, France, Belgium, Luxembourg and the Netherlands to sign the Brussels Treaty in March 1948, committing the participating members to a system of collective self-defence.

NATO

Just over one year later, in April 1949 the system of collective self-defence would evolve into the signing of the North Atlantic Treaty in Washington by Belgium, Canada, Denmark, France, Iceland, Italy, Luxembourg, the Netherlands, Norway, Portugal, the United Kingdom and the United States.

NATO was significant not just because of the commitment of collective self- defence but also because of the fact that American involvement provided an important balance of power within Europe.

The OEEC

The Organisation for European Economic Co-operation (OEEC) was also established in April 1948 with the purpose of supervising the Marshall Aid programme which provided just under $12.5 billion in aid to Europe between 1948-1951 Based on an intergovernmental method of co-operation, the OEEC managed to lower trade barriers among European nations and provide the first step towards European economic co-operation.

Despite its success many countries argued that the OEEC lacked the necessary supranational structures to bring long-term changes to the economic and political situation in Western Europe.

However, not all European nations were prepared to accept the loss of national sovereignty that supranational co-operation required. Britain, Portugal and many of the Scandinavian countries favoured intergovernmental co-operation that did not lessen the authority of elected governments.

The Hague Congress

The Hague conference in May 1948 was prompted by the desire of federalists to form a constitution which would form the basis for European co-operation. Out of the discussions that took place arose the Council of Europe, formed in May 1949, of which Britain was a member.

The Council of Europe met (still does meet) on an annual basis and provided the first opportunity for the rehabilitation of West Germany when it became a member in 1950.

The Coal and Steel Community

In 1950, the Schuman Declaration (after the French Foreign Minster Robert Schuman stated 'the French Government proposes that Franco-German coal and steel production should be placed under a common High

16

Authority in an organisation open to other countries of Europe'. The significance of the declaration lay in the desire of France to forfeit an amount of national sovereignty through the creation of new supranational structures in an effort to create peace and as such it is generally regarded as a key action in the construction of Europe.

Belgium, Italy, Luxembourg and the Netherlands responded positively to the Schuman Declaration. Germany was particularly enthusiastic. However, Britain was not so enthusiastic. The final outcome of the negotiations was the formation of the European Coal and Steel Community, which was formally signed in Paris on 18th April 1951 by representatives of Belgium, France, Germany, Luxembourg, Italy and the Netherlands. The process of ratification was completed by the end of June 1952. The underlying objective of the treaty was to foster 'economic expansion, growth of employment and a rising standard of living' in the member states by means of creating a common market in coal and steel that would be managed by joint institutions on the basis of agreed policies. Such policies would embrace consumption, development, expansion, prices, production, trade and the economic and social conditions of employees working within the industry. One impact of these policies was the immediate abolition of all coal and steel import and export duties and the removal of all national subsidies for these commodities.

Although the Treaty concentrated on coal and steel the preamble demonstrated the desire of the participants to move beyond coal and steel and to create a wider Community in the longer term. The idea was to create a federal prototype. Therefore, the significance of the ECSC lay in the capacity for European integration to progress beyond initiatives such as the Council of Europe. The ECSC offered a new form of organisation where nation states agreed to surrender an element of their sovereignty to a supranational institution.

The Treaties of Rome

In June 1955 the foreign ministers of the six member states of the ECSC met in Messina, Italy, to discuss proposals for further European integration, of which the fields of transport and atomic energy were considered possible options. The outcome was that the six ministers passed a resolution that noted that 'The Governments of the Federal Republic of Germany, Belgium, France, Italy, Luxembourg and Netherlands believe that the time has come to make a fresh advance towards the building of Europe. They are of the opinion that this must be achieved, first of all, in the economic field'. Out of these meetings was created the EEC and Euratom (European Atomic Energy Community, which took effect on 1st January 1958.

In the next chapter we will look at the development of the European Community since 1957 and the Treaties of Rome.

Chapter 2

The European Community from 1957 Onwards

The main principle, or objective, of the European Community is the establishment of a common market. All Member States of the EC will be directly affected by the common market, as will individuals in those states.

One of the earliest cases that reinforces this is Van Gend en Loos v Nederlandse Administratie Der Belastinge (case 26/62) 1963. In this case, Van Gend en Loos, a firm of importers were required to pay customs duty on a product imported from Germany, under a law adopted after the creation of the (then) EEC. The importers challenged the payment on the basis that the extra duty infringed Article 25 of the Treaty (see below) which prohibited the introduction of new customs duties. The Dutch Court referred the question to the European Court of Justice under Article 234. It was held that the EC is a new legal order in international law, on behalf of which states have limited their sovereign rights and whose subjects comprise not only states but individuals. Article 25 of the treaty produces direct effects in the relationship between the Member States and their subjects, creating individual rights which the national courts must protect.

The background to the European Community from 1957 onwards

As we have seen, the present European Community (EC) and the European Union (EU) have their origins in the European Economic Community (EEC) created by the Treaty of Rome in 1957. This original treaty provided the basis for a customs union and what is known as the common market, which is the free movement of goods, people, services and money for the original six signatory states. Those states were Germany, France, Italy, Belgium, the Netherlands and Luxembourg. In addition, as we have also seen, the same states also formed the European Coal and Steel Community (ECSC) and the European Atomic Energy Authority (Euratom).

Later, in 1973, the United Kingdom, Denmark and Ireland took up membership. The UK's membership was against the well-documented backdrop of dissent. The United Kingdom has enacted the European Communities Act in 1972 to give effect to its obligations under EC law. Later on, other countries joined, Greece 1981, Spain 1986, Portugal 1986 and Austria, Sweden and Finland in 1995. As we will see, many other countries have gained membership since 1995.

The main institutions of the EU

There exist five main institutions which carry out the main tasks of the European Community, all of which will be examined in detail later in the book:

- The Council of Ministers-an ad hoc body of ministers from the Member states responsible for the adoption of legislation

- The Commission-a permanent body which proposes legislation and also has a monitoring role in relation to the implementation of EC law

- The European Parliament

- The Court of Justice-this court is the final authority on matters of European Community law, assisted by the Court of First Instance

- The Court of Auditors

The Treaties

The main point about the European Community Treaty, in its various stages, is that it is an integral part of the legal system of the Member States and, as such, must be applied in their courts.

One of the earliest cases challenging the legitimacy of the EC Treaty is that of Costa v ENEL (Case 6/64) 1964. In this case the nationalised Italian Electricity Company (ENEL) had been created in 1962. Costa refused to pay his bill on the grounds that the nationalisation infringed the Italian Constitution and also various provisions of the treaty. It was held by the European Court of Justice, in this case, that the transfer by Member States from their domestic legal systems to the EC system of rights and

21

responsibilities carries with it a permanent limitation of their sovereign rights, against which a later unilateral act incompatible with EC law cannot prevail.

The original European Economic Community Treaty was amended in 1986 by the Single European Act (SEA). It was also further amended in 1993 by the Treaty on European Union (Maastricht Treaty) and the 1997 Treaty of Amsterdam (ToA). The Single European Act created the mechanism to complete the single, or internal, market. This is an area without internal frontiers within which goods, services, people and money can circulate freely.

The Treaty on European Union created a structure based on three pillars:

1) the EC
2) the Common Foreign and Security Policy
3) Police and Judicial Co-operation

The first pillar, the EC, is governed by law under the EC Treaty, the second and third pillars are administered through intergovernmental co-operation. The Maastricht Treaty provided for both political and monetary union (EMU). The single currency came into effect on January 1st 1999.

The United Kingdom, through protocols annexed to the treaty, opted out of EMU and, at the time of the Maastricht Treaty, of the Agreement on Social Policy (known as the Social Chapter) which established a legal base for certain types of employment protection.

Ratification of all member states of the Maastricht Treaty was completed in 1999, May 1st, this being the date that the Treaty Amendments came into force. The Treaty of Amsterdam introduced into the treaty an Employment Chapter, requiring member states to co-ordinate their economic policies, focussing on growth and employment.

The European Court of Justice now has jurisdiction in certain areas relating to police and judicial co-operation (the third pillar). The Social Chapter was incorporated into the body of the revised Treaty following the change of government in the UK in 1997. Article 13 of the Treaty provides the basis for action to combat discrimination on the grounds of gender, race, religion, sexual orientation or disability. Sanctions can be imposed on member states for infringements of human rights.

The Schengen Agreement

The revised treaty also incorporated the **Schengen Agreement.** Member states agreed to relax border formalities on the movement of people. The United Kingdom and Ireland have opted out of this part of the treaty. Following the signing of the Treaty of Nice in February 2001, the Treaty came into force on February 2003.

The Treaty of Nice

The Treaty of Nice paved the way for a significant enlargement of the European Community, taking in a large number of mainly Eastern European states. As a result of the newly enlarged EU, with a virtual doubling of its Members, the current EU is a different body to the previous one. Major changes are required and are now in process. The Treaty of Nice sets out principles and methods to change the system as the EU expands. For example, changes to the composition of the Commission and weighted voting in the council applied from 2005 and changes in the number of MEP's applied from the elections in 2004.

In December 2001, the Laeken European Council issued a Declaration leading to the setting up of the European Convention, which involved existing Member States and applicant states in discussion about the EU. The Convention on the Future of Europe took place in March 2002 and closed in March 2003. The resultant treaty arising from these sessions was rejected, due to continuing differences over qualified voting in the Council.

Ten new Member States joined the EU on May 1st 2004- the Czech Republic, Estonia, Latvia, Cyprus, Lithuania, Hungary, Malta, Poland, Slovenia and Slovakia. In the absence of a new treaty, institutional changes were governed by the provisions of the various acts of accession and the Treaty of Nice.

In October of 2004, in Rome, agreement was eventually reached, and signed, on a Constitutional Treaty for the EU. The Treaty will not become binding until it has been ratified by all Member States. This has so far been a very long and difficult process. If it is ever ratified, the new Constitutional Treaty will lead to a number of changes, including the fusion of the three (above outlined) pillars into a single entity, namely the European Community.

In 2007, further Member States have been added, Romania and Bulgaria with plans to add more, notably Albania. The UK has adopted a different set of criteria in relation to these countries with regard to the right to work and settle in the UK.

****

Chapter 3

Institutions of the European Union

3.1 The European Parliament

The European Parliament is the directly elected parliamentary body of the European Union. Together with the Council of the European Union (see later) it forms the bicameral legislative branch of the Union's institutions.

The Parliament, along with the Council, forms the highest legislative body within the Union. The Parliament represents approximately 496 million citizens of the European Union. Its members are known as Members of the European Parliament They are elected every five years, since 1979, by universal suffrage and sit according to political allegiance. Prior to 1979, they were appointed by their national parliaments. Parliament is composed of 785 MEP's. This figure will eventually drop to around 740 after the 2009 election.

MEP's in the Parliament are currently organised into eight different political groups, with 15 non-attached, or independent, members, also known as *non-inscrits* These groups are not, by definition, European Political parties but are composed of them. In some cases there is a single party forming its own group in other cases there are coalitions.

There are three main groups (of more than 100 MEP's). The European People's Party-European Democrats (EPP-ED) is the largest with 278 MEP's. It is a centre right alliance of the European People's Party (Christian Democrats) and European Democrats. The Party of European Socialists (PES) is the second largest group with 201 MEP's. The third largest is the Alliance of Liberals and Democrats for Europe (ALDE) with 103 MEP's. There are a further five groups, including the greens, nationalists and fringe groups. To be recognised, groups have to include 20 members or more from one-fifth of member states.

The political parties comprising the parliamentary groups are themselves comprised of national parties. The British Conservative Party, for example, forms part of the European Democrats, which in turn forms part of the EPP-ED group.

The President of the European Parliament

The President of the European Parliament (its speaker), currently Hans-Gert Pottering (EPP), elected in 2007, presides over a multi-party chamber, the two largest groups being the European People's Party-European Democrats (EPP-ED) and the Party of European Socialists (PES). The European Parliament has two meeting places, Brussels and Strasbourg. The Secretariat of the European Parliament is based in Luxembourg.

Brief history of the European Parliament

The European Parliament began as the 'Common Assembly' of the European Coal and Steel Community (ECSC). It was a consultative assembly of 78 parliamentarians drawn from the national parliaments of member states, having no legislative powers.

The Common Assembly renamed itself the 'European Parliamentary Assembly' with the creation of the European Economic Community and Euratom in March 1958. It served all three communities, while the Commission and Council has separate bodies for each. The three merged in 1967 and the body was renamed again to the current 'European Parliament'. In 1979, its members were directly elected for the first time. After the first election, the Parliament held its first session in July 1979, electing Simone Veil as president. Thereafter, the membership of the European Parliament has simply expanded whenever new nations have joined. Recent treaties have set the cap on membership for a single election to 750.

Powers of the European Parliament

The European Parliament and the Council are two chambers in the bicameral legislative branch of the European Union, with legislative power being officially distributed equally between the two chambers. However, as mentioned, there are key differences between the EU Parliament and the Council and the national legislatures. Neither the Parliament nor the Council have the power of legislative initiative. In Community matters this is a power reserved for the European Commission (the Executive). Whilst Parliament can amend and reject legislation, and also make proposals and recommendations, the Commission has to draft a bill before anything can become law. The Parliament has a significant amount of indirect influence, through non-binding resolutions and committee hearings. Parliament must approve all development grants, including grants for overseas countries.

Legislative procedure

The European Parliament, together with the Council, with whom powers are shared equally, will amend and approve or reject all draft legislation introduced by the Commission. Both chambers must agree before draft legislation becomes law. This is known as the co-decision procedure. In addition to co-decision, Parliament, as the only directly elected democratic institution, has, ultimately, greater control over legislation than other institutions. This is a situation that has evolved naturally.

Budget

The legislative branch officially holds the Union's budgetary authority. The EU's budget is divided into compulsory and non-compulsory spending. Compulsory spending results from EU Treaties (including agriculture) and international agreements. All other spending is non-compulsory. The Council has the final say on compulsory spending and the parliament on non-compulsory spending. The various institutions draw up budget estimates and the Commission consolidates them into a final draft budget. Both the Council and Parliament can amend the budget with the Parliament adopting or rejecting the budget at its second reading. The signature of the Parliaments President is necessary before the budget becomes law.

Control of the Executive

The President of the European Commission is proposed by the Council and that proposal has to be approved by Parliament. Therefore, Parliament has the right of veto. Following approval of the Commission President, the members of the Commission are proposed by the President in accord with the member states. They are then approved or rejected by Parliament.

Parliament also has the power to censure the Commission as a body, once they are in power with a two-thirds majority.

Powers of supervision

The Parliament has general powers of supervision, mainly granted by the Maastricht treaty. The European

Ombudsman is elected by the Parliament. The Ombudsman deals with all public complaints against the EU institutions. Parliament has the power to set up a commission of enquiry, can call all other institutions to answer questions and, if necessary to take them to court if they are in breach of EU law or Treaties. Parliament also has powers over the appointment of the Court of Auditors (see later) and the President and the Executive Board of the European Central bank. The President of the Bank is obliged to present an annual report to Parliament.

****

3.2 The European commission

The European Commission is the executive branch of the European Union. It is a cabinet government of 27 Commissioners lead by a Commission President. The current Commission, known after its President as the 'Barroso' Commission took office in 2004 and is serving a five-year term. The Commission is responsible for proposing legislation, implementing decisions, upholding the Union's treaties and the general day-to day running of the commission.

History

The Commission originated in 1951 with the establishment of the European Coal and Steel Community. In 1958, with the creation of two new communities, two sister bodies were established under the terms of the Treaties of Rome. These were the Commission of the European Economic Community and the Commission of the European Atomic Energy Community. The three bodies co-existed until 1st July 1967 where, by means of the Merger Treaty, the three bodies were combined into a single administration, called the Commission of the European Communities.

The Commission was set up from the start to act as an independent supranational authority separate from governments. Although the members come from national governments they are bound to act independently. This is

33

in contrast to the Council which represents governments and the Parliament which represents citizens.

Executive power of the Union is held by the council, representing governments. That power is conferred upon the Commission by the council and may be withdrawn. Powers are outlined in Articles 211-219 of the EC Treaty.

The Commission differs from the other institutions in that, over the European Community, it alone has legislative initiative. Only the Commission can make formal proposals for legislation. Bills cannot originate in the legislative branch. However, it shares that right with the Council, and has no right over police and judicial co-operation in criminal matters. Once legislation is passed, it is the commission's responsibility to ensure that it is implemented, by member states or through the agencies of the European Union. In adopting the necessary technical measures the Commission is assisted by committees made up of representatives of member states.

The Commission is also responsible for the implementation of the EU budget, ensuring, along with the Court of Auditors (see later) that EU funds are correctly spent. In addition, the commission has a duty to see that Treaties and law are upheld. In this role it is known informally as 'Guardian of the Treaties'. Although foreign policy is mainly under the control of member states, the Commission also provides external representation for the union. It is responsible for negotiating international trade agreements.

The Electoral College

The Commission President is nominated by the European Council, who is then officially elected by the European Parliament. Following their appointment, the President appoints a number of Vice-Presidents. The Commission itself is composed of a 26 member college of Commissioners. Each member is appointed by a state, however, does not represent it. The President delegates portfolios between each of the members and the body as a whole must be approved by Parliament before they take office.

Organisation

The Commission is based mainly in Brussels, in the Berlaymont. The Commission also operates out of other buildings in Brussels and Luxembourg. The Commission is divided into departments known as Directorates-General (DG's). Each covers a specific policy area or service such as translation or external relations. Each DG is headed by a Director General who is responsible to a Commissioner. DG's prepare proposals and if adopted by a Commissioner it goes forward to Parliament and Council for consideration.

Legitimacy

While the Commission is the Executive branch, the candidates are chosen primarily by the 27 national governments, meaning that it is hard for the Commission to be thrown out by the voters The legitimacy of the Commission is mainly drawn from the vote of approval that is required from Parliament along with Parliament's powers to sack the body.

Future of the European Commission

In June 2007, the details of a Reform Treaty were agreed. The reforms proposed a number of changes, notably to the number of Commissioners, seeking a reduction. From 2014 only two-thirds of the Member States would have the right to representation. The representation would be rotated equally between all states and no state would have more than two in any single Commission. The Commission would also include the new High Representative of the Union for Foreign Affairs and Security Policy, as one of the Vice Presidents, replacing the External Relations Commissioner. There are a number of other minor changes contained within the reform proposals.

****

3.3 The Council of the European Union

The Council of the European Union, informally known as the Council of Ministers, is one of two legislative institutions of the European Union, the other being the European Parliament. The Council, together with the Parliament, forms the highest legislative body within the Union. It is composed of 27 national ministers (one per state). The ministers are accountable to their national electorates. The Union's law is limited to specific policy areas and does not override national law.

The Council does not have a single President, the role is rotated between each member state every six months (known as 'the Presidency'). Another powerful position is the Secretary General who is also the representative of the Union's foreign policy.

History of the Council

The Council first appeared in the European Coal and Steel Community (ECSC) as the 'Special Council of Ministers' With the Treaties of Rome in 1957, two new council's were established, The Council of the European Economic Community and the Council of the European Atomic Energy Community. With the Merger treaty of 1965, the three bodies were combined into a single Council of the European Communities. In 1993, the body became the Council of the European Union (following the Maastricht Treaty).

Powers

The Parliament and Council are, essentially, two chambers in the bicameral legislative branch of the European Union, with legislative power being officially distributed equally between both chambers. However, neither the Parliament nor Council can initiate legislation. As mentioned earlier, this power lies with the Commission.

In addition to its legislative functions, the Maastricht Treaty (Article 202) outlines further functions for the Council:

- Ensure co-ordination of the general economic policies of the Member States.

- Have power to take decisions

- Confer on the Commission, in the acts which the council adopts, powers for the implementation of the rules which the Council lays down. The Council may impose certain requirements in respect of the exercise of these powers. The Council may also reserve the right, in specific cases, to exercise directly implementing powers itself. The procedures referred to above must be consonant with principles and rules laid down in advance by the Council, acting unanimously on a proposal from the Commission and after obtaining the opinion of the European Parliament.

In effect, the Treaty outlines that the Council performs the following functions:

- Legislation-the Council passes EU law on the recommendations of the European Commission together with the European Parliament using the Co-decision procedure

- Approval of the EU budget-the Council and the Parliament must agree on the budget

- Foreign and defence policy-while each member state is free to develop its own foreign and defence policy, the Council seeks to achieve a common policy for its member states

- Economic policy-the Council also seeks to achieve a common economic policy for the member states

- Justice-the Council seeks to co-ordinate the justice system of the member states, especially in areas such as terrorism.

The Council also officially holds the executive powers of the Union, conferring it upon the Commission and able to withdraw it by Article 202 of the Single European Act which states 'The Council confers on the Commission powers for the implementation of the rules it lays down. It may impose certain requirements in respect of the exercise of these powers. In specific cases, it may reserve the right to exercise implementing powers directly'.

Legislative and budgetary authority

There are various legislative procedures used in the union. The Co-decision procedure is the most common, which gives the Parliament and Council equal powers in that legislation can be amended or rejected by both chambers. Other procedures include co-operation, meaning the council can overrule Parliament if it is unanimous and the Consultation and Assent procedures which require consultation of the Parliament only.

The Council votes in one of three ways: unanimity, simple majority or qualified majority. In most cases, the Council votes on issues by Qualified Majority Voting, which means that there must be a minimum of 255 votes out of 345 (73.9%) and a majority of member states.

The legislative branch officially holds the Union's budgetary authority. The EU's budget is divided into compulsory and non-compulsory spending. Compulsory spending is that resulting from EU Treaties (including agriculture) and international agreements. The rest is non-compulsory. While the Council has the last word on compulsory spending, Parliament has the last word on non-compulsory spending.

The institutions draw up the budget estimates and the Commission consolidates them into a draft budget. Both the Council and the Parliament can amend the budget, both have to agree for the budget to become law. In addition to the budget, the council also co-ordinates the economic policy of members.

Configuration

The Council is a single entity, legally, but it is in practice divided into several different councils that meet in Brussels, each dealing with a different area. Each council is attended by a different type of minister, relevant to that council. Therefore meetings of the council in its agriculture and fisheries formation are attended by the agriculture ministers of each state. There are, at the moment, nine different formations of the Council:

- General Affairs and external Relations (GAERC) this is the most important of the formations and is composed of ministers for foreign affairs

- Economic and Financial Affairs

- Agriculture and Fisheries

- Justice and Home Affairs Council (JHA)

- Employment, Social Policy, Health and Consumer Affairs Council (EPSCO)

- Competitiveness

- Transport, Telecommunications and Energy

- Environment

- Education, Youth and Culture (EYC)

In addition to the above, the Political and Security Committee (PSC) brings together Ambassadors to monitor international situations and define policy within the ESDP, particularly in times of crisis.

****

3.4 The European Council

The European Council is similar to a configuration of the Council, operating in the same way and sharing the same presidency system but is composed of the national leaders (heads of state). The body's purpose is to define the general 'impetus' of the Union. The European Council also deals with major issues such as the appointment of the President of the European Commission who also takes part in the body's meetings.

Administration

The General Secretariat of the Council provides the infrastructure for the administration of the Council's business. The Secretary General of the Council is head of the Secretariat.

Voting

As discussed, the Council is composed of national ministers for the relevant topic of discussion, with the ministers representing their states. Different states have different voting weights, as follows:

- Germany, Italy, France and the United Kingdom-29 votes

- Spain and Poland-27 votes

- Romania-14 votes

- Netherlands-13 votes

- Belgium, the Czech Republic, Greece, Hungary and Portugal-12 votes

- Austria, Bulgaria and Sweden-10 votes

- Denmark, Ireland, Lithuania, Slovakia and Finland-7 votes

- Cyprus, Estonia, Latvia, Luxembourg and Slovenia-4 votes

- Malta-3 votes

****

3.5 The European Court of Justice

Summary

The Court of Justice of the European Communities, known as the European Court of Justice is the highest court of the European Union (ECJ). It has the ultimate say on matters of European Union law in order to ensure equal application across member states.

The ECJ was established in 1952 and is based in Luxembourg city. The court is composed of one judge per member state although only 13 judges can hear a case at any one time. Cases are heard in the 'Grand Chamber' and is led by a president.

The court is assisted by a lower court, the Court of First Instance dealing with certain issues of law. There are two other courts dealing with other responsibilities, the Civil Service Tribunal (EU employees) and the Court of Auditors (EU accounts).

History of the European Court of Justice

The court was established in 1952 by the Treaty of Paris (1951) for the European Coal and Steel Community. It was initially set up with seven judges. It became an institution when the Treaties of Rome established the European Economic Community (EEC) and the European Atomic Energy Community (EURATOM). Although all three communities were separate, under the

Convention of March 1957 they shared some common institutions, these being the Parliamentary Assembly and the Court. It was with this that the Court of the ECSC became the Court of Justice of the European Communities.

The European Court of Justice is the highest court of the European Union in matters over which it has competency. It adjudicates on matters of interpretation of European Community law, most commonly:

- Claims by the European Commission that a member state has not implemented a European Union Directive or other legal requirement

- Claims by member states that the European Commission has exceeded its authority

- References from national courts in the EU member states asking the ECJ questions about the meaning or validity of a particular piece of EU law. The Union has many languages and competing political interests and so local courts often have difficulty deciding what a particular piece of legislation means in a given context. The ECJ will then give its ruling which is binding on the national court.

Organisation of the ECJ

The Court of Justice is made up of 27 Judges and 8 Advocates General (as at January 2007). If the Court requests the Council of the European Union, acting unanimously, can increase the number of Advocates General. The Judges and Advocates General are appointed by common accord of the governments of the member states and hold office for a renewable term of six years. They are chosen from legal experts who possess the requisite qualifications to hold high office in their own countries. Each member state of the European Union has the power to nominate one judge.

The President of the Court of Justice is elected from among the judges every three years. This is a renewable term. The President presides over hearings and deliberations, directing judicial business and administration. He or she will also assign cases to the chambers for enquiries and appoints a judge as a rapporteur.

Advocates General

Advocates general play a special role within the Courts of Justice. They are neither judge nor prosecutor, yet they assist with each case and deliver their opinions on questions.

The Advocates-General assist the Court in its task. They deliver in open court opinions in all cases, save as other wise decided by the Court where a case does not raise any new points of law.

Registry

The Court appoints the registrar for a period of six years, after which he or she may be reappointed. They have the same court duties as the registrar of a national court, but also act as the secretary general of the institution. The Court may also appoint one or more assistant registrars. The Registrar is responsible for the overall administration of the Court, its financial management and its accounts, assisted by an administrator.

Plenary sessions and chambers

The Court of Justice may sit as a full Court, in a Grand Chamber (13 judges) or in chambers of three or five judges. It sits in a grand chamber when a Member state or a Community institution that is party to the proceedings so requests, or in particularly important or complex cases. Other cases are heard by a chamber of 3-5 judges. The presidents of the chambers of five judges are elected for three years, the Presidents of the Chambers of three judges for one year.

Jurisdiction

It is the responsibility of the Court of Justice to ensure that the law is observed in the interpretation and application of the Treaties of the European Union and of the provisions laid down by the competent Community institutions. To enable it to carry out that task the court has wide jurisdiction to hear various types of action. The

Court has competence, inter alia, to rule on applications against Member States for failure to fulfil obligations, references for a preliminary ruling and appeals against decisions of the Court of First Instance.

Seat

Both the Court of Justice and the Court of First Instance have their seats in Luxembourg

****

3.6 The European Court of Auditors

The European Court of Auditors has as its mission 'to audit independently the collection and spending of European Union funds and, through this, assess the way that the European institutions discharge these functions'.

The Court of Auditors checks that all the Union's revenue has been received and all its expenditure incurred in a lawful and regular manner and that the EU budget has been managed soundly. The Court was established on 22nd July 1975 by the Budgetary Treaty of 1975. The Court started operating as an external community audit body in October 1977. Since the Treaty of Maastricht the European Court of Auditors has been recognised as one of the institutions of the European Communities.

The Court has one member from each EU country, appointed by the Council for a renewable term of six years. Even after enlargement there will still be one member per EU country but, for the sake of efficiency, the Court can set up Chambers (with a few members) to adopt certain types of report or opinion.

The Members of the Court of Auditors are all specifically qualified for the role of auditors, qualifying and working within there own country. They are chosen for their competence and independence and work full time for the Court.

The members elect one of their number as president for a term of three years.

Function

The Court's main role is to check that the EU budget is correctly implemented. Its work helps ensure that the EU system operates efficiently and openly. To carry out its task, the Court investigates the paperwork of any organisation handling EU income or expenditure. It carries out on-the-spot checks if necessary. From its investigations it will draw up reports which it will present to the Commission.

One of the Court's key functions is to help the budgetary authority (the European Parliament and Council) by presenting them every year with a report on the previous financial year. The comments made in this report play a very important role in Parliament's decision whether or not to approve the Commission's handling of the budget.

The Court of Auditors also gives an opinion before the EU's financial regulations are adopted.

The Court has over 700 qualified staff assisting it in its task. Of these about 250 are auditors who are divided into teams or 'audit groups'. They prepare draft reports on which the Court takes decisions. The Court has no legal powers of its own. If fraud is discovered or any other irregularities they will pass the information to the EU bodies responsible so that action can be taken.

For twelve years in a row the Court of Auditors has refused to sign off the EU accounts, stating that there have been irregularities. Examples of fraud have been monies disappearing in the Balkans and Russia. In addition, the Court suggested that the EU staff were abusing the disability system on a large scale. The work of the Court is ongoing to ensure a clear and transparent system.

****

Chapter 4

The Free Movement of Goods

The free movement of goods is at the very core of the European Community and Union today. The free movement of goods is essential to the creating and running of the customs union and the common market and provides the infrastructure for the rest of the community. The main reason for creating this common market is to ensure that Europe can compete with existing and emerging markets around the world. In addition, another objective is to ensure that member states become interdependent and interconnected and remain on peaceful terms.

Competition law within the EU is vital to the effectiveness of this internal market and we will be discussing this later.

Legislative provisions

There are four main groups of provisions in the EC Treaty connected with the free movement of goods:

1) customs duties and charges having equivalent effect (Articles 23-25)

2) the Common Customs Tariff (Art 26-7)

3) The use of national taxation systems to discriminate against goods imported from other member states (Art 90)

4) quantitative restrictions or measures having an equivalent effect on imports and exports (Arts 28-30)

Customs duties and charges having equivalent effect (Articles 23-25)

These sections of the Treaty concern not just customs duties which hinder free trade, but also any financial barriers which have an equivalent effect, whatever they are termed.

Article 23 states that the Community must be based on a customs union, with a common customs tariff, involving the prohibition of all customs duties on imports and charges having similar effect. This provision covers all 'trade in goods', with goods being defined by the Court of Justice in Case 7/68 Commission v Italy (Art Treasures Case) as 'products that can be valued in money and which are capable, as such, of forming the subject of commercial transactions'. The definition was extended in Case 45/87 Commission v Ireland (Dundalk Water Supply) to include the provision of goods within a contract for provision of services.

Article 25 prohibits customs duties or charges having equivalent effect and applies to both imports and exports.

In Cases 2 and 3/62 Commission v Luxembourg the Court of Justice held that:

A duty, whatever it is called and whatever its mode of application, may be considered a charge having an equivalent effect to a customs duty, provided that it meets the following criteria:

a) it must be imposed unilaterally at the time of importation or subsequently;

b) it must be imposed specifically upon a product imported from a member state to the exclusion of a similar national product; and

c) it must result in an alteration of price and thus have the same effect as a customs duty on the free movement of products.

The Common Customs Tariff (Art 26-7)

The Common Customs Tariff (CCT) which is also referred to as the 'common external tariff' imposes a single tariff for all imports and is set by the Commission. Once a product has been imported into the EU it is then in free circulation and further tariffs cannot be imposed on the product.

The use of national taxation systems to discriminate against goods imported from other member states (Art 90)

Article 90 (1) provides that no member state shall impose directly or indirectly on the products of other member states any internal taxation of any kind in excess of that imposed directly or indirectly on other domestic products (i.e. VAT). Article 90(2) further provides that no member state shall impose on the products of other member states any internal taxation of such a nature as to afford indirect protection to other products. One case where Article 90 was shown to be effective was case 57/65 Lutticke v Hauptzollamt Saarlouis.

Taxation was defined in case 90/97 Commission v France (Reprographic Machines) as a general system of internal dues applied systematically to categories of products in accordance with objective criteria irrespective of the origin of the products.

Article 90 seeks to outlaw both direct discrimination and indirect discrimination in tax regimes. Direct discrimination is where imports and domestic products are deliberately treated differently and indirect discrimination, on the face of it, imposes the same rule on both domestic and imported products, but the end result is that the imported product is in fact disadvantaged. In Case 28/76 Molkerei-Zentrale Westfalen v Haupzollamt Paderborn the Court of Justice ruled that the words 'directly' or indirectly' were to be construed broadly and embraced all taxation which was actually or specifically imposed on the domestic product at earlier stages of the manufacturing process. It is also capable of including taxes on raw materials and to the assessment of tax.

Quantitative restrictions or measures having an equivalent effect on imports and exports (Arts 28-30)

A quantitative restriction is a measure restricting the import or export of a given product by amount or value.

Restrictions or obstacles to free movement of goods and services are caused mainly by divergent national laws regulating products and trade. Whereas quantitative restrictions are straightforward, either bans or quotas, it is the extent to which member states can insist that imported goods comply with national standards in the face of the attempt to create a single unified market, that causes the real problem.

Article 28 lays down a general prohibition on quantitative restrictions and measures having equivalent effect and Article 29 extends that provision to imports. Article 30 provides:

The provisions of Articles 28 and 29 shall not preclude prohibitions or restrictions on imports, exports or goods in transit justified on the grounds of:

- public morality, public policy or public security

- the protection of health and life of humans, animals or plants

- the protection of national treasure possessing artistic, historic or archaeological value

- the protection of industrial and commercial property.

However, the above may not be used as a means of arbitrary discrimination or a disguised restriction on trade between member states.

In Case 249/81 (Buy Irish) a buy Irish campaign was administered by the Irish Goods Council, a registered private company. However, because the Irish government mainly sponsored the campaign to buy Irish products, generally controlling the process, Article 28 was held to apply. Effectively, they were in breach. In another case, Apple and Pear Development Council v Lewis, a government sponsored development council was under a duty not to run an advertising campaign to encourage purchase of domestic fruit at the expense of imported products.

There have been many arguments by traders against national rules restricting trade and, in the seminal Case of Keck and Mithouard (case 267-68/91) 1993, the Court of Justice was able to clearly define the position. This Case concerned the French prohibition of goods, at a loss, which was argued to be a restriction of sales contrary to Article 28. The Court of Justice stated that:

In view of the increasing tendency of traders to invoke Article 28 of the Treaty as a way of challenging any rules whose effect is to limit their commercial freedom even where such rules are not aimed at products from other member states, the court considers it necessary to re-examine and clarify its case law on this matter.

The Court considered that traders had been using Community law to try to challenge laws which were not aimed at restricting imports but restricted the sales of all goods, domestic and imported. The court then stated that it considered that selling or marketing arrangements did not come within the concept of Article 28. The Court of Justice held that:

Contrary to what has been previously been decided, the application to products from other member states of national provisions restricting or prohibiting certain selling arrangements is not such as to hinder directly or indirectly, actually or potentially, trade between member states within the meaning of the Dassonville judgement provided that those provisions apply to all traders operating within the national territory and provided that they affect in the same manner, in law and in fact, the marketing of domestic products and of those from other member states.

In the Dassonville Case, Case 81/74 Procureur du Roi v Dassonville, the term 'measures having equivalent effect' was held to include 'all trading rules enacted by a Member state which are capable of hindering, directly or indirectly, actually or potentially, intra-community trade. This particular case concerned criminal proceedings in Belgium against a trader who imported scotch whiskey in free circulation in France into Belgium without having a certificate of origin from the British customs, thus infringing Belgian customs rules. The Court of Justice held that:

The requirements by a Member State of a certificate of authority, which is less easily obtainable by importers of an authentic product, put into free circulation in a regular manner in another Member State, than by importers of the same product coming directly from the country of origin, constitutes a measure having equivalent effect.

Overall summary

The overall aim of the policy of the free movement of goods is to achieve the circulation of goods without customs, duties, charges or other financial restrictions, or indeed any restrictions: the promotion of unlimited trade and to remove from the member states the control over export and import matters.

****

Chapter 5

Free Trade Area

This involves the removal of customs duties between member states, however the members of a free trade area decide themselves their external policies and any duties payable by third party countries wishing to export goods to those countries.

Customs Union

Following on from the above is the creation of the customs union which builds on the above by creating a common external tariff, presenting a common position. The same duties are imposed on goods entering the customs union regardless of where they are imported from.

The Common Market

The Common market is the next stage which develops the above with the free movement of the factors of production (goods, persons and capital) and a competition policy. The common market not only provides for the elimination of duties regarding goods originating in other member states, but also regarding goods originating in third countries which are in free circulation in the common market and on which customs duties have been paid. The external duties are fixed by the Community for goods imported from outside of the Community and a single set of common tariffs (Common Customs Tariffs) is adopted in trade relations with the outside world.

Economic Union

An economic union is a combination of all of the above plus the harmonization or unification of economic, monetary, and fiscal policies including the creation of a common currency controlled by a central authority. The final step is the full political union in a federal state.

Developments to 2007

Whilst the goals are clear, as with all massive undertakings the degree to which a common market has been established is doubtful as there are a number of obstacles in the path and a considerable amount of case law still arising. However, twelve countries to date, representing less than half of the member states, have gone further and established an economic and monetary union with a European Central Bank and a common currency (The Euro).

Integration methods

The integration of what were a number of separate markets is to be achieved by two main strategies, positive and negative integration. Negative integration is the removal of existing obstacles to free movements, such as removing national rules and practices which stand in the way of harmonization. Positive integration is achieved by the modification of existing national laws and institutions through the creation of new laws.

Negative integration

This is the outlawing of national rules and practices which obstruct the fundamental free movement regimes. In the EU legal order, this form of integration is found in the statutory attempt to ensure the free movement of goods under Articles 25 to 31, workers under Articles 39-42, the provision of services and establishment under Articles 43-55, and capital under Articles 61-69.

The prohibition of discrimination, the general rule contained within Article 12, is very important in this area because prior to the establishment of the common market, free movement of goods could be restricted solely on the basis of the country from which the goods came.

The prohibition of discrimination

Article 12 provides 'Within the scope of application of this treaty, and without prejudice to any special provisions contained therein, any discrimination on the grounds of nationality shall be prohibited'.

Discrimination can appear in the form of direct discrimination. It is not restricted to intentional discrimination but also unintentional discrimination if the effect of a rule is nevertheless to discriminate against imports.

Positive integration

Positive integration involves the introduction of new laws and regulations to ensure that there is an equal playing field for imported and domestically produced goods by the introduction of new community wide laws or the setting up of institutions to ensure European wide regulation and control, for example the European Central bank and the single currency. It also includes the harmonization and approximation of national legislation by replacing multiple and divergent national rules or, where relevant, the absence of national law, with a single EU rule which advances free trade.

In the EU, harmonization is achieved by legislative intervention empowered by specific Treaty bases, for example the free movement of workers.

There are different forms of harmonization that can have effect: total or complete harmonization, whereby one rule is enacted for the whole community and precludes member states from legislating in the same area; optional harmonization which incorporates the idea that producers need only follow the provisions of a directive where they intend to trade goods across an EU member state frontier;

minimum harmonization, which is the establishment of a minimum standard but which does not mean that member states cannot go further and insist on higher domestic standards. This would not apply to imported goods.

Alternatives to legislative harmonization

Rather than harmonize, which, by its very nature can be a long process, an alternative led by judicial development is that of 'mutual recognition' of standards. This principle was one of two established by the Court and made prominent in the case of Cassis de Dijon, (Case 120/78 Rewe-Zentral AG v Bundesmonopolverwaltung fur Branntwein) 1978.

The case revolved around a prohibition on the marketing in the Federal Republic of Germany of spirits with less than 25% alcohol content, which included Crème de Cassis de Dijon, a blackcurrant alcoholic liqueur containing only 15-20% alcohol. The ban applied to all low alcohol liqueurs regardless of nationality of origin. The German rationale was that lower alcohol drinks would lead to alcohol tolerance thus leading to health problems later on. The lower alcohol also provided a price advantage for the imported products which was unfair and would force down alcohol rates of drinks and thus quality contrary to usual manufacture. However, the actual result was the effective ban of French imports, indirectly. The Court of Justice held that there was no reason why, provided that they had been lawfully introduced and marketed in one of the member states, alcoholic beverages should not be introduced without restriction into another member state.

This decision essentially holds that if a product is lawfully produced in one state, meeting the health and safety requirements of that state, then states into which the product is imported should accept those standards and thus the products as equivalent of domestic standards and products. They should not ban them as not complying with health and safety requirements which differ.

****

Chapter 6

Competition Law

The purpose of competition law is to regulate the activities of (mainly) commercial undertakings to curb the excesses of the free market or to put right situations that arise in an unregulated free market which would be harmful to parties in the system or, in the extreme, the system itself.

Competition law regulation was regarded as a necessary and essential element in the building of the Community and Union. The EU also needed a competition policy to ensure the maintenance of the free market. The whole basis of the EU is premised on the desire and need to promote integration and create a single unified free market. A competition policy within the EU prevents companies from creating rules and obstacles to trade which unfairly disadvantage competitors.

Outline of EU competition policy

The broad policy objective was to both maintain and stimulate/encourage competition for the benefit of the community and its citizens, to achieve and open a unified market and the integration of the community, to encourage economic activity amongst small and medium size enterprises, and to maximise efficiency by allowing the free flow of goods and resources.

EC competition rules are generally designed to intervene to prevent agreements which fix prices or conditions or the supply of products, to prohibit agreements which carve up territories and to prevent abuses of market power which have the effect of removing real competition and controlling mergers which would also remove competition. As with the free movement of goods, the rules cover all items capable of forming the subject of commercial transactions.

The aims are set out in the preamble and Articles 2-4 of the EC Treaty. The preamble refers to the 'removal of existing obstacles calls for concerted action in order to guarantee steady expansion, balanced trade and fair competition'.

Article 2 of the Treaty refers to' establishing a Common Market and an economic and monetary union by implementing the common policies...referred to in Articles 3-4, to promote...a harmonious and balanced development of economic activities.

Article 3(1)(g) of the EC Treaty lists among the activities of the Community

'A system ensuring that competition in the internal market is not distorted'.

Article 10 is also a general principle of law supporting the argument that competition law also applies in respect of the member states and not just undertakings so that they are prohibited from encouraging or requiring acts or conduct by companies which may distort competition in the Community.

The broad aims are then expanded as follows:

- One relating to business activities, i.e. legal persons

- One relating to anti-dumping measures

- One relating to the activities of the member states

The rules concerned with the private undertakings are then subdivided into two provisions:

- Article 81 for agreements between cartels involving more than one entity and

- Article 82, concerned with dominant positions, dealing predominantly with one entity but also applicable to one or more undertakings.

Applying and interpreting competition law

The Commission is given the task under article 85 of the EC Treaty to ensure that competition in the Community is not distorted. The application of the rules by the Commission and the interpretation of rules by the Court of Justice have been applied in the light of the objectives of the Treaty. In Case 6 and 7/73 Commercial Solvents v Commission, the Court of Justice held:

'The prohibition in Articles 85 and 86 (now 81 and 82) must be interpreted and applied in the light of Article 3(f) (now 3(g)) of the Treaty which provides that the activities of the Community shall include the institution of a system ensuring that competition is not distorted, and Article 2 of the Treaty which gives the Community the task of promoting 'throughout the Community harmonious development of Community activities'.

Article 81

Article 81 deals with restrictive practices. It sets out the prohibitions and details of the consequences of the failure to observe the prohibition. It also provides a framework by which exemptions from the prohibitions can be obtained. Article 81 (1) EC prohibits agreements between undertakings, decisions by associations of undertakings, and concerted practices which may affect trade between the member states, and which have as their objective or effect the prevention, restriction or distortion of competition within the common market.

Article 81(2) provides that any agreements or decisions prohibited pursuant to Article 81 shall be automatically void. Article 81(3) concerns exemptions to the basic rules.

The object and effect of reducing competition

An agreement or practice is prohibited if it has the effect or object of restricting competition. Article 81(1) lists as particular examples of such agreements, which have as their object, the restriction of competition. This list includes:

a) directly or indirectly fix purchase or selling prices or any other unfair trading conditions

b) limit or control production, markets, technical developments, or investment

c) share markets or sources of supply

d) apply dissimilar decisions to equivalent transactions with other trading parties, thereby placing them at a competitive disadvantage: and

e) make the conclusion of contracts subject to the acceptance by the other parties of supplementary obligations, which by their nature have no connection with the subject of such contracts.

Trade between member states

To be caught by the provisions of Article 85, the practice complained of must be capable of effecting Community trade if an agreement or similar is to be caught in breach of Article 81. Trade is given a wide definition and encompasses the production and distribution of good's, trade in agricultural produce, the services sector and any other form of trade.

In case 56 and 58/4 Consten and Grundig, the Court of Justice stated that this phrase (trade) is intended to set the boundary between the areas covered by Community law and the law of the member states. It held that the question to be asked is whether it is probable in law or fact that the agreement in question may have an influence, direct or indirect, actual or potential, on the pattern of trade between member states to hinder the attainment of a single market.

The case was concerned with exclusive territorial sales licences which served to encourage the volume of trade. Consten Grundig had granted a distributor a sole representation agreement for the whole of France, Saar and Corsica. The distributor undertook not to sell similar articles liable to compete with the goods of the contract and not to deliver either directly or indirectly, for or to other countries, from the contract territory. A similar prohibition was imposed on concessionaires from other territories. The result was to grant absolute territorial protection, and to insulate the French market against parallel imports. The result in this case was that it actually promoted trade. The Court of Justice held that the fact that an agreement encourages an increase, even a large one, in the volume of trade between states is not sufficient to exclude the possibility that the agreement may affect trade between member states.

In Case 23/67 Brasserie de Haecht SA v Wilkin and Wilkin, the brewery had entered into a contract whereby they furnished the Wilkins café and had granted several loans. The agreement stipulated that the Wilkins were obliged to obtain all their supplies of liquor, beer and soft drinks for the café and for their own personal use exclusively from the brewery. They had purchased supplies of liquor from other undertakings and the brewery had sought to rescind the contract and claim repayment of the loans, return of furniture and damages.

The Tribunal de Commerce asked the Court of Justice whether to judge the agreement on its own or in the light of all such agreements. The Court ruled that indeed the 'economic and legal context' had to be taken into account, such as in this case the fact that the arrangement tying the café proprietors to receiving their beer and other drink supplies from one brewery was one which was extensively used, and the extensive use of such contracts would adversely affect competition in the Community at large. The Court further ruled that in order to satisfy the 'capable of affecting trade between member states' requirement:

It must be possible for the agreement, decision or practice, viewed objectively to appear to be capable of having some influence, direct or indirect on trade between member states, partition the market, and hampering the economic interpretation sought by the treaty. When this point is considered the agreement, decision or practice cannot therefore be isolated from the others of which it is one.

Therefore, if it forms a series of agreements, a single contract should not just be considered on its own.

Exemptions from Article 81 (1)

Certain agreements have been deemed by the Court of Justice and the Commission not to fall within the category of a 'restriction of competition'.

Objective necessity

There are cases where the restrictions are objectively necessary for the performance of a particular type of contract. Clauses in agreements which are indispensable to prevent the know-how and assistance provided by a franchisor, for example, from benefiting competitors and clauses which implement the control necessary for the preservation of the identity and reputation of the organisation represented in the trade mark, do not constitute restrictions on competition within the meaning of Article 81 (1).

High commercial risks

The Court of Justice has held that where the commercial risk undertaken by a distributor, licensee or franchise is so great, some exclusivity must be conferred on him to induce him into the market. Case 55/65 STM v Maschinenbau is an example of this. In this case, the French Company La Societe Technique Miniere purchased thirty seven earth levelling machines, and were given exclusive rights for the territory of France. The agreement with the producers, Maschinenbau Ulm stipulated that they could only sell other goods to compete with these levelling machines with the consent of the suppliers. The agreement left STM entitled to export the machines.

The Court of Justice held that in order to assess the effect of the agreement on competition, examination should take place of the severity of the clause granting the exclusive right: the nature and quantity of the products which are the subject matter of the agreement: the position of the grantor and the concessionaire on the market for the product in question: the number of parties to the agreements: and the possibilities left for other commercial currents upon the same products by means of re-exports and parallel imports.

The Court held that due to the high cost of the product and specialised nature, the agreements would not breach Article 81.

Quality control

It is seen that cases involving selective distribution systems such as those which benefit the consumer in terms of safety of electrical goods and to maintain employment in an important industry would not breach Article 81.

The *De Minimis* Doctrine

The doctrine of *de minimis* means that some agreements which affect competition may not be caught by Article 81 because they do not have any significant effect on trade. This doctrine was first created in Case 5/69 Volk v Verwaecke where Volk granted an exclusive dealership to Verwaecke for the supply of washing machines in the Belgian and Luxembourg markets. Verwaecke undertook to place a monthly order for eighty appliances, with Volk undertaking to protect that territory for parallel appliances. A dispute followed relating to the agreement and the Court of Justice held that an agreement falls outside of the scope of Article 81(1) when it has only an insignificant effect on the market, taking into account the weak position that the parties have on the market in question.

In relation to this, the Commission produced an updated 'Notice on Agreements of Minor Importance which do not appreciably restrict competition' setting out the criteria which will be used when determining whether a practice will affect trade between member states. The basic criteria are that the undertakings have less than 10% market share in the Community as a whole. The threshold for vertical agreements is 15% of market share.

Article 82 and the abuse of a dominant position

Article 82 applies where individual organisations have a near monopoly position or share an oligopolistic market

76

with a small number of other companies and take unfair advantage of this position to the detriment of the market, other companies and ultimately consumers.

Article 82 states 'Any abuse by one or more undertakings of a dominant position within the common market or in a substantial part of it shall be prohibited as incompatible with the common market insofar as it may affect trade between member states'. Article 86 then goes on to give specific examples of such abuse.

The leading case arising out of Article 82 is that of Case 27/76 United Brands v Commission. This case arose out of a complaint by a number of other banana exporters about the activities of this particular company. Some of the facts were as follows: bananas are picked and transported whilst green; they only begin to ripen after they have been gassed, which usually takes place at the country of destination; there was a requirement that distributors did not sell bananas whilst green.

In addition, they charged different prices to different distributors. One particular distributor was not supplied because they also advertised another brand.

As a result of the various activities of United Brands the Commission considered that they had breached Article 82 and imposed a fine of 1 million units of account (the forerunner of the Euro). UBC appealed to the European Court of Justice.

The issues for the ECJ to consider were the proof of dominance in the market and the abuse of this which affected trade. A dominant position was defined as:

'A position of economic strength enjoyed by an undertaking which enables it to hinder the maintenance of effective competition on the relevant market by allowing it to behave to an appreciable extent independently of its competitors and customers and ultimately consumers'.

The Court looked at issues such as the definition of the product and the relevant product market, the relevant geographical market, market share and dominance and the abuse of the dominant position. The Court decided that UBC had infringed Article 82 in that it had required its distributors not to sell bananas while green and had charged distributors in different member states different prices without justification. UBC had also refused to supply a Danish company with Chiquita bananas because they had advertised another brand.

The enforcement of Community Competition law

The Community has quite extensive independent enforcement powers under Regulation 1/2003, which replaced Council Regulation 17, and which contains extensive enforcement rights. This regulation empowers the Commission to carry out its function of ensuring that the provisions of the EC Treaty are applied, to address undertakings, decisions and recommendations for the purpose of bringing to an end infringements of Articles

81-82 and to enforce these by way of fines and periodic payments.

In addition, the Regulation sets out the powers and duties of the Commission in the conduct of investigations of competition law abuses, which can be prompted by individuals and companies, the member states or on the Commissions own initiative.

Regulation 1/2003 Articles 1-16 are mainly concerned with the respective powers of the Commission and national authorities, interim measures, cooperation between the Commission and national authorities and with the procedure of the declarations by the Commission that the agreement largely infringes the Treaty or is exempt from the Treaty provisions.

Articles 17-21 concern the powers of the Commission in conducting investigations, Articles 23-28 concerned with sanctions available to the Commission in the case of infringements which have been established by it and the rights of parties under investigation.

Article 20 is significant in that it gives the Commission sweeping powers to undertake all necessary investigations including the right of officials to examine books, take copies of records, ask for oral explanations and also enter the premises of undertakings including new extended powers under Article 21 to search the homes of directors and managers and others where it is suspected that records relevant to an investigation are stored there. This can happen without the consent of the relevant undertaking provided that it is authorised in advance by the Commission.

All decisions taken by the Commission under Regulation 1/2003 are subject to review by the Court of First Instance under Article 230 EC with the possibility of a further appeal to the European Court of Justice.

Private enforcement

As with other areas of EC law, the enforcement of Community rules can also take place by individuals before the national courts via the vehicle of direct effects. One case which illustrates this is Case C-453/99 Courage v Crehan which concerned a pub tenant tied to an agreement to buy beer from Courage Brewery alone. He claimed this was a breach of Article 81 and claimed damages. As a party also tainted by the agreement, the UK court was minded to dismiss the claim but nevertheless made a reference to the Court of Justice under Article 234 EC. The Court of Justice, in looking back at the importance in securing enforcement rights for individuals and the effectiveness of Community law held that Competition rules were fundamental rules in the EC, and if the agreement was in breach of Article 81 and not able to be exempted, it was void and could not be relied upon by anyone, including a party to the agreement.

The Court held that, in line with case developments in other areas, in order to ensure the effectiveness of

Community law, the procedural rules of the member states should not deprive individuals of rights in the absence of a Community regime. That matter was ultimately up to member states courts but there should be no absolute bar to an action where the contract was found to breach Article 81.

The party in the Crehan v Courage Case did eventually win damages for breach of Article 81.

Community merger control

Mergers Regulation 139/04 sets out controls relating to mergers and acquisitions. This Regulation replaced all former Regulations. Mergers are termed 'concentrations' under the Regulation.

Regulation 139/04 provides the legal basis of Community policy and control of mergers and acquisitions.

Regulation 139/04 establishes a division between large mergers with a European dimension over which the Commission will exercise supervision, and smaller mergers which will fall under the jurisdiction of national authorities. The concept of concentration was set out in a Commission Notice (OJ 1998 C/66/2).

Article 1 states that the Regulation applies to mergers and takeovers with a Community dimension, applies where there is a worldwide turnover of more than 5,000 million Euros and an aggregate Community wide turnover of each of at least two of the undertakings of more than 250 million Euros. A Community dimension may pertain if:

a) the combined aggregate worldwide turnover of all the undertakings is more than 2,5000 million euros;

b) in each of at least three member states, the combined aggregate turnover of all the undertakings is more than 100 million euros;

c) in each of at least three member states, the aggregate turnover of at least two of the undertakings concerned is more than 25 million euros; and

d) the aggregate Community wide turnover of at least two of the undertakings concerned is more than 100 million euros.

However, if each of the undertakings concerned achieves more than two-thirds of its aggregate Community wide turnover within one and the same member state, a concentration will fall outside of the scope of the Regulation, and the merger will be subject to national rather than Community control.

Article 2 provides the power of review to determine whether mergers are compatible with the common market. The creation or strengthening of such a position will be incompatible with the common market where it would significantly impede competition in the common market as a whole or a substantial part of it. The Commission is required to take into account the following matters when making an appraisal:

- the need to preserve and develop effective competition within the common market

- the structure of all the markets concerned

- the actual or potential competition from undertakings located within or without the European Community

- the market position and economic and financial powers of the undertakings concerned

- suppliers and users access to supplies and the markets

- legal barriers to enter the market

- supply and demand trends for the relevant goods and services

- the interests of intermediate and ultimate consumers and the development of technical and economic progress provided that it is to the consumers advantage and does not prove an obstacle to competition.

When a merger is found by the Commission not to impede competition, it will be declared compatible with the common market, Article 2 (2). The member states, however, retain the power to veto mergers in particularly sensitive areas of their economies, providing this is compatible with the general requirements of Community law.

Article 3 defines a concentration to include mergers, acquisitions of direct or indirect control of undertakings by persons already controlling at least one undertaking, partial mergers, and merger like joint ventures. It docs, however, exclude from the scope of the Regulation, coordination of market behaviour of firms which remain independent of each other. Such coordination, if adverse to competition in the common market would fall within the scope of Articles 81 or 82.

One recent case would seem to go against this view however. In joined cases C-68/94 France v Commission and C-30/95 Societe Commerciale des Potasses et de lazote (SCPA) v Commission, the Court of Justice determined that a merger Regulation may also apply to collective dominance. The case concerned a proposal that potash companies in Germany be concentrated, thus creating a de facto monopoly in the German market and a dominant position with the French company (SCPA) within the Community market. To obtain the Commission's approval the parties agreed to certain conditions relating to cooperation between the dominant firms and the distribution of the products in the markets identified.

Enforcement of Regulation 139/04

Article 4 (1) requires the notification of a concentration with a Community dimension within one week after the conclusion of the agreement, the announcement of the public bid, or the acquisition of a controlling interest, whichever of these should occur first. Fines for a failure to notify can be imposed up to a maximum of 50,000 Euros.

Article 7 (1) provides that a concentration with a Community dimension shall not be put into effect before notification or in the three weeks following notification. The validity of transactions in securities on stock exchanges shall not be affected.

Under Article 10 (1) the decisions to open proceedings referred to in Article 6 must be taken within one month of the day following receipt of the notification. Article 6 provides that the Commission is under a duty to examine all notifications as soon as they are received, and to notify decisions to undertakings and national authorities without delay.

Article 10 (3) requires that a decision that a concentration is incompatible with the common market must be taken within four months of the decision to open proceedings. During this period, the parties to the proposed concentration will be free to propose changes to their merger in order to avoid a negative decision.

Where the Commission has found a proposed concentration to be incompatible with the common market, it may require the separation of the undertakings or the cessation of joint control or any other action deemed appropriate.

So far, the Regulations have not been extensively used to prevent mergers. However, one exception was the proposed merger of Aerospatiale, Alenia and de Havilland (MO53) which was prohibited under the Regulation for the reason that the merger would have had an unacceptable impact on customer choice and the balance of competition in the EU.

Article 13 confers the power to undertake 'all necessary investigations on the Commission, including the powers for officials to examine and take copies of records and other books, to ask for oral explanations on the spot and to enter any premises, land or other.

The Regulation also allows for the imposition of fines for failure to notify, supplying incorrect or misleading information and for obstructing an investigation.

****

Chapter 7

Citizenship of the European Union-Free Movement of Persons/Labour

In the first instance, free movement of people within the EU related to the free movement of workers and self-employed people only. However, free movement of persons has become a much wider concept, although the original treaty Articles on free movement have altered little since 1957. Free movement has become inextricably linked to European citizenship over the years.

The free movement of persons within the EU is firmly set within the economic part of the EU Treaty, concerned with a basic definition of the internal market and outlined in Article 14 and not within the social policy section of the treaty as outlined in the next chapter.

The legal framework

Treaty provisions

Referring to the main goals outlined in Article 2 of the treaty, Article 3 provides that 'For the purposes set out in Article 2, the activities of the Community shall include, as provided in this Treaty and in accordance with the timetable set out therein:

a) an internal market characterised by the abolition, as between member states, of obstacles to the free movement of goods, persons, services and capital.

Article 14 provides that in paragraph 2 that 'the internal market shall comprise an area without internal frontiers in which the free movement of goods, persons, services and capital is ensured in accordance with the provisions of this treaty'.

The Treaty Articles outlining the basic requirements to facilitate the free movement of economically active people are: Articles 39-42 for workers, Articles 43-48 for those wishing to establish and Articles 49-55 for those wishing to provide services.

Article 39(1) for workers provides that freedom of movement for workers shall be secured within the Community and that such freedom of movement shall entail the abolition of discrimination based on nationality between workers of the member states regards employment, remuneration and other conditions of work and employment.

Article 39 (3) described the rights of workers but subjects those rights to the limitations on grounds of public policy, public security or public health, as further set out in the new directive 2004/38. The rights are:

a) to accept offers of employment actually made;
b) to move freely within the territories of the member states for this purpose;
c) to stay in the member state for purposes of employment in accordance with the provisions governing the employment of nationals of that state laid down by law and regulation of administrative action;
d) to remain in the territory of a member state after having been employed in that state and governed by Regulation 1251/70.

Article 39(4) provides that 'The provisions of this Article shall not apply to employment in the public service'.

For establishment, Article 43 provides that the freedom of establishment shall include the right to take up and pursue activities as self-employed persons and to set up and manage undertakings, in particular companies and firms.

For the provision of services, Article 49 provides that 'restrictions on freedom to provide services within the Community shall be prohibited in respect of nationals of member states who are established in a State of the Community other than that of the person for whom the services are intended'.

Discrimination

A fundamental right relating to free movement is that there should be no discrimination on the grounds of nationality. Article 12 EC, which prohibits discrimination on the grounds of nationality, has been applied in a number of cases, which will be discussed below.

The Court of Justice has stated that the concept of discrimination not only covers direct discrimination in which different rules apply to nationals, and non-nationals, but also covers covert discrimination or indirect discrimination which leads to the prejudicial treatment of non-nationals.

Indirect discrimination was demonstrated in Case 33/88 Allue Coonan v University of Venice. The applicants after five years of employment as foreign language lecturers, were informed that they could not be retained under a 1980 Italian Decree which limited the duration of employment of foreign language lecturers. Not all the foreign language lecturers were non-national, some 25% were nationals, therefore there was no dissimilar treatment, i.e. no overt discrimination. Although the rule applied regardless of nationality it nevertheless mainly affected the non-nationals who made up the majority of lecturers. It was held by the Court of Justice to be discriminatory where such limitations do not exist in respect of other workers.

Who benefits from the basic rights

Two basic definitions have to be established: nationality and whether the person concerned is a worker or self-employed by establishing or providing services; or other wise entitled to remain in the member state.

Nationality

For workers and self-employed, the right to move freely and obtain other benefits, especially those rights which can be taken up by members of the worker's family, is initially dependant on being defined as a national of one of the member states. Article 39 secures freedom for workers of the member states. Establishment under Article 43 and services under Article 49 refers to the rights of nationals of the member states to either establish or provide services in other member states. Companies which are registered in one of the member states fall within the scope of the rights afforded under this Article.

The determination of member state nationality is a matter for each of the member states as expressly stated in Declaration No 2 on nationality attached to the Treaty on European Union which provides that nationality shall be settled solely by reference to the National law of the member state concerned. This was upheld in Case C-192/99 Manjiit Kaur in which the Court of Justice held that it is for each member state to lay down the conditions for the acquisition and loss of nationality. It is not, however, necessary for the members of a workers family to be member state nationals to obtain benefits as will be seen in the secondary legislation and case law outlined below.

Status as a worker or self-employed

In order for a person to benefit personally, or their family to benefit from the rights arising under Articles 39-55 the person needs to be classified as a worker or self-employed. The definition of these categories is a matter for the Community as opposed to the national states.

Worker

The Court of Justice, in the Case 75/63 Hoekstra v BBDA, provided a limited definition of a worker. 'A worker is any employed person, irrespective of whether he is wage earning or salaried, blue collar or white collar, an executive or unskilled labourer'. The Court of Justice has since expanded the definition in a series of cases to include part time workers, work seekers, and in certain circumstances those undertaking a course of study.

One case, Case 53/81 Levin v Minister of Justice, concerned part time work. This examined the value of work that a person does before they can be classed as a worker. The woman plaintiff, a British woman, worked in Holland as a chambermaid for 20 hours a week and her earnings were below subsistence level in the Netherlands. The Dutch government argued that because she was a part-time worker earning below the official subsistence level she was not a 'favoured EEC Citizen' and therefore could not benefit from the provision of EEC law guaranteeing freedom of movement of workers. The Court of Justice held that these considerations were irrelevant to her status as a worker, and stated that whether she was full-time or part-time, she was entitled to the status of worker provided that the work was genuine and effective and not so infinitesimal as to be disregarded. The essential defining characteristic of work is that it is an activity of an economic nature.

The term 'worker is, however, wider than just referring to those in employment and in certain circumstances also applies to those who are seeking work, and those who having lost one job involuntarily, are capable of taking another.

Those seeking work

Certain rights are retained by workers who lose a job. It was thought that those who lose employment retain rights for a period of up to three months, where they could draw benefits. This was set out in Regulation 1408/71, Article 69. It was then argued before the Court of Justice that after this time a person could be deported. Several important cases have examined this.

Case 316/85 Marie-Christine Lebon. The Court of Justice held that those in search of work are not entitled to receive workers benefits. Miss Lebon no longer lived with her parents who were ex-workers therefore she did not qualify for benefits as a dependant of a worker. The question was raised as to whether she qualified for workers benefits if she was looking or intended to look for work. The Court of Justice held that the benefits provided by legislation on free movement were only for those in actual employment not for those who come in search of work but have not found it. She could temporarily be classified as a worker but not for the purpose of benefits.

Case C-292/89 Antonissen, clarifies how long the temporary status entitles a person to look for work. The UK wished to deport Antonissen, who had been convicted of possession and intention to supply cocaine. The UK Courts asked the Court of Justice if they could deport. UK legislation gave EC citizens six months in which to find employment. Antonissen was in the country for over three years without work before his conviction. The Court held that, after the expiry of a reasonable period, depending on the circumstances, a person may no longer be afforded the status and benefits of worker under the Community law and may be lawfully deported by the member state.

Worker training, education and benefits

There are those who no longer work but are engaged in a course of study. Several cases have defined this right. The leading case is Case 39/86 Lair v Universitat Hannover, in which a French national employed in West Germany was refused a grant by the university for a maintenance award and training fees because she had not worked in the country continually for at least five years and therefore whilst at university was not a worker. It was stated in the case that the period at university would lead to a vocational qualification and that the time at university represented a break in employment only. The Court of Justice held that since there was no fixed definition of worker, there was nothing to say that the definition must always depend on a continuing employment relationship. Certain rights have been guaranteed to workers after employment has finished, e.g. the right to stay and social security rights. This could also apply to university training provided that there was a link or continuity between the previous work and university. If this was the case then the university support could be considered one of the social rights coming within Regulation 1612/68.

A case which contrasts this is Case 197/86 Brown v Secretary of State for Scotland. The Scottish Education Department refused Brown a grant for university. He had worked for eight months prior in the UK as a precursor to university and gained the status of worker. The Court of Justice held that, whilst university training is to be regarded as mainly vocational it was only covered by Article 12 EC generally outlawing discrimination. This covers tuition fees but not the maintenance grant, therefore a person who enters employment for eight months and did so as a precursor or requisite to attend university did not retain the status of worker to obtain a grant.

Other cases have questioned this judgement. The outcome is that the prime consideration is that definitions of what constitutes vocational training and the link to work are crucial for the determination of status as a worker and the consequent rights and benefits that flow from that.

The establishment and provision of services

The self-employed are granted rights under the treaty to move to another member state to establish permanently or on a long-term basis. (Articles 43-8) or to provide services temporarily (Articles 49-55). The definitions for the personal scope of establishment and for the provision of services are much more straightforward than for workers as the primary Treaty Articles have laid down the basic concepts which have not been the subject of any significant interpretation by the Court of Justice. Article 43 deals with rights of freedom of establishment as the right to enter another member state and stay on a long term or temporary basis, to take up and pursue activities as a self-employed person and to set up and manage undertakings. This includes legal as well as natural persons.

Services under Article 49 envisages a temporary state of affairs and appearance in a host state would only be for a limited period to provide specific services. There would be no permanent or professional presence in the host state or intention to provide it. The concept of services is defined by Article 50 as those 'provided for remuneration, in so far as they are not governed by provisions relating to freedom of movement of goods, capital and persons' in particular. Article 50(d) specifically included activities of industrial and commercial characters and those of craftsmen and the professions.

The provision of services is a wider category and is associated with banking, finance, legal and insurance services and also modern technology.

Rights of entry, residence and exit

The rights to enter and move freely to take up employment are governed by a combination of Articles 39 (3) Regulation 1612/68 and Directive 2004/38 Articles 4-14, although much of the case law is associated with the now repealed Directive 68/360 Articles 1-6 and 8.

Articles 1 and 2 of the Regulation 1612/68 provide the right to take up employment in the host state under the same conditions as nationals without discrimination. Regulation 1612/68 Article 3(1) permits imposition on non-nationals of conditions relating to linguistic ability required by the nature of the post to be filled. One case that illustrates this is Case 379/87 Groener v Minister for Education in which the Court of Justice upheld an Irish requirement that teachers in Ireland be proficient in Irish as part of a public policy to maintain and promote the Irish language and culture.

Directive 2004/38 provides the rules to regulate the conditions by which workers can leave one member state and enter the territory of another. Article 4 provides that exit states are obliged to allow nationals and their families with a valid passport to leave with an exit visa or other formality. The exit state is obliged to issue a passport or ID card. Article 5 states that entrance states cannot demand an entry visa or equivalent documents from EC nationals. They can, however, require to see valid documents and visas from non-EC family members.

Article 6 permits the right to enter, travel and live in a host member state for a period of up to three months by an EU citizen. His or her family is not restricted to the economically active but to any EU citizen without any other conditions other than the requirements to hold valid identity and/or visa documents. The right to reside for a period of longer than three months is made conditional on being engaged in a gainful activity, being self-employed or even as a recipient of services with comprehensive sickness insurance cover.

As well as residence permits for family members, a registration certificate can be demanded which must be granted to any worker who produces a passport and certificate of proof of employment. Members of the workers family must also be given a registration certificate on production of a passport or proof of dependence. In Case 459/99 MRAX the Court of Justice considered that it was disproportionate and therefore prohibited, to send back a third country national married to a national of a member state not in possession of a valid visa where he is able to prove his identity and conjugal ties and there is no evidence to show that he presents a risk to the security, health or the public.

The new Directive reflects previous case law and provides that the failure to register and comply with registration requirements may render the person involved liable to proportionate and non-discriminatory administrative sanctions only

Procedural safeguards

There is a right to remain in a member state pending a decision either to grant or refuse a residence permit, except in emergency situations. Article 30 provides that the grounds for deportation must be precisely and clearly stated and the person involved has a right to be informed of the decision unless security is involved. These rights were summed up in Case 115-116/81 Adoui and Cornauille v Belgian State in which two French women, described as waitresses, had their residence permits withdrawn by the Belgian authorities on the grounds that their personal conduct justified it. They were, in short, engaged in prostitution which was seen as contrary to public policy. A reference was made to the Court of Justice, which held that the public policy proviso does not allow expulsion where similar conduct by nationals does not incur similar penalties. It was noted that Belgian prostitutes were tolerated not prosecuted.

Article 30(3) provides the right to be notified of any decision to expel or the refusal of a permit, and should also state the minimum period given to leave the country which cannot be less than one month in any circumstance. Article 31 provides for appeal against decisions.

Education and carer rights

Article 12 of Regulation 1612/68 provides that children of a national of a member state shall be admitted to the general educational, apprenticeship and vocational training courses under the same conditions as nationals. Case 9/74 Casagrande had already extended the right under Article 12 to include not just access to educational facilities but equality of measures intended to facilitate educational attendance and in case C-7/94 Gaal, the Court of justice extended the right under Article 12 to an independent and over 21 year old child of a migrant worker who had been employed in another member state. Gaal was the Belgian son of an EC worker in Germany who had since died. Gaal was attending university and had applied for a grant to undertake an eight month period in the UK, but this was refused on grounds that he was over 21 and was not dependant and was therefore denied his rights as a descendant of an EC worker. The Court of Justice held that he still fell within the scope of Article 12 of the Regulation as the definition of a child was not subject to the same definition as in Articles 10 and 11. Article 12 extends to all forms of education including university and must include older children no longer dependant on their parents. The case was, however, decided on the basis that the child must have lived at some time with a parent who was an EC worker and thus derived his rights in this manner.

In relation to carers, two cases have defined this right. In Case 413/99 Baumbast and R v Home Secretary the non-EU national mothers would otherwise have been deported if the Court had not held that the children had the right to be cared for where the original basis of their right to stay in the UK had disappeared, one through divorce and the other because there was no longer a Community national working in the UK or other member state. In Case C-200/02 Chen where the child in question, a Community national born to two Chinese nationals who had not even moved from one member state to another and was below school age was the reason the Chinese nationals gained the right to stay in the UK.

The Right to remain

Article 39 (3) (d) provides the right to remain after retirement or incapacity and applies also to members of the family even if workers die, and to whom Article 7 (2) of Regulation 1612/68 continues to apply. The right to remain now also includes permanent residence rights. Article 12 provides that the Union citizens death or departure from the host member state shall not affect the right of residence of family members who are nationals of a member state and also to non-member state family members who were living with the union citizen for at least one year before his or her death. Any children retain the right to attend educational establishments also. Article 13 provides that divorce, annulment of marriage or termination of the partnership or relationship shall not affect the right of residence of a Union citizens family members who are nationals of a member state and also those who are not nationals of a member state. The latter category is subject to the requirement that the marriage or partnership has lasted at least three years, one being in the host state or where the spouse or partner has custody of family children or is warranted by particular family circumstances. The right to remain under Articles 12 and 13 are further dependant on the persons considered not being a burden on the host state.

Article 16 provides that Union citizens who have resided legally for a continuous period of five years in the host member state shall have the right of permanent residence there and that continuity of residence shall not be affected by temporary absences not exceeding six months a year or by longer absences not exceeding twelve months at a time for important reasons, such as pregnancy or illness. Paragraph 1 also applies to family members who are not nationals of a member state and have resided with the Union citizen in the host member state for at least five years. Article 17 provides that this period may be reduced in cases of death or injury of the union national. In respect of family members who are not nationals of a member state Article 18 provides that they shall acquire the right of permanent residence after residing legally for a continuous period of five years in a host member state.

Restrictions on grounds of public policy, security and health

Member states are able to restrict entry and deport EU nationals on the grounds set out under Article 39(3) which are public policy, security and health.

Articles 46 and 55 EC subject establishment and provision of services to the same derogation as workers.

Articles 27(2) requires that measures taken on the grounds of public policy or public security shall comply with the principle of proportionality and shall be based exclusively on the conduct of the person concerned and provides that serious criminal convictions shall not in themselves constitute grounds for taking such measures. It further provides that the personal conduct of the individual concerned must represent a genuine, present and sufficiently serious threat affecting one of the fundamental interests of society.

In Case 41/74 Van Duyn v The Home Office, the Court of Justice held that restrictions on the grounds of public policy must be interpreted very strictly and be subject to judicial review. In this case, a Dutch woman obtained a position as a secretary with the Church of Scientology in the UK but was refused entry by the Home Office on the grounds that public policy declared the Church to be socially harmful. Miss Van Duyn claimed that the decision was not made on personal conduct but on the conduct of the group.

The Court of Justice held that personal conduct must be an act or omission to act on the part of the person concerned and must be voluntary. It need not, however, be illegal or criminal to offend public policy. The Court further held that present association reflecting participation in the activities and identification with the aims of a group may be considered a voluntary act and could therefore come within the definition of conduct which hands back some of the discretion to the member states to determine whether an individuals association in a group constitutes personal conduct.

Public service

Status as Public Service

Article 39(4) exempts employment in the public service from the provisions of Article 39. It applies to entry to the public service but not to the actual employment. The Court of Justice has stressed that a strict interpretation of the Article is essential as there are a wide variety of interpretations of what constitutes public service across member states.

Receiving services

Freedom of movement may also exist for those who are not workers or self-employed. Basically, right to free movement is not wholly underpinned by economic activity.

The concept of services has been expanded to those who, rather than actively pursue an economic activity, instead are passive in receipt of services of an economic activity. Whilst there is nothing to confirm this category in the Treaty, it was expressly mentioned in Article 1 of Directive 64/221 but not in directive 2004/38 (the main directive covering rights of general movement).

Services can either be received by both movement to another member state or by receiving services from another state in the home state. Initially, cases which concerned this arose from the areas of tourism and education.

In Case 286/82 Luisi and Carbone v Ministero del Teauro, two Italian nationals were prosecuted under Italian Currency regulations for taking money out to pay for tourist and medical provisions abroad. These were held by the Court of Justice to be payments for services and thus coming under the provisions of EEC Treaty, payments also being a fundamental freedom of the Community and the case was covered by Articles 59,60, and 7 (now 49, 50, and 12).

In Case 293/83 Gravier v City of Liege, a decision to charge foreign students a fee for vocational training courses but not nationals was claimed to be contrary to Community law (Articles 12, 49 and 150). This was upheld in the case which confirmed that university study was, for the most part, vocational training in EC law terms and that Community nationals have a right to equal access to receive that training even where fees are paid by the host state.

****

Chapter 8

Social Policy and Equality

There has been a theme of equality and non-discrimination throughout this book. Articles 2 and 3 seek to prohibit discrimination and promote equality. Article 12 (nationality) and Article 13 also contain powers to prohibit discrimination. Other Articles are 39, 43 and 50 which provide for equal treatment of workers and the self employed, Article 86 (public undertakings) Article 90 (taxation), Article 137 (equality of men and women in the work environment) and Article 141 (equal pay).

Article 12 which prohibits discrimination on the grounds of nationality is the fundamental basis for the integration of workers into the Community.

The legislative framework

Treaty Articles

Article 141 (formerly 119) (equal pay for equal work) has formed the basis whereby the principle of non-discriminatory treatment has been expanded into areas other than equal pay. Now, following the Treaty of Amsterdam, EC Treaty references to the promotion of equality are more extensive. The ToA introduced as one of its main goals, outlined in Article 2 'equality between men and women' and has added a new final sentence to Article 3 which reads: 'In all the activities referred to in this Article, the Community shall aim to eliminate inequalities and to promote equality between men and women'.

Secondary legislation

The European Summit Meetings of 1972-3 and in particular the Paris Summit in 1972 asked the Commission to produce proposals for a Social Action Programme, as the first of what turned out to be a number of action programmes. The first report was published in 1974, dealing with a number of measures such as redundancy and transfer of undertakings. Three directives dealing with equality between men and women were adopted: The Equal pay Directive 75/117, the Equal Treatment Directive 76/207 and the Social Security Directive 79/7.

A second Social Action Programme was commenced in 1982 which led to the enactment of Directive 36/378 on equal treatment in occupational pensions and Directive 86/613 on equal treatment of the self-employed and protection of self employed women during pregnancy and motherhood.

In 1989, The Charter of Fundamental Social Rights of Workers (The Social Charter) was adopted by eleven of the twelve (not the UK) member states. The next step was the EC Treaty Amendment by the Maastricht Treaty which attached an agreement and protocol on social policy (known as the Social Chapter) to the Treaty to which fourteen of fifteen member states signed up (not the UK). This led to the enactment of further directives including the Parental leave Directive 96/34, the Burden of Proof in Sex Discrimination cases Directive 97/80 and the Part Time Workers Directive 97/81.

Article 141 and the principle of equal pay

Article 141 (ex 119) originally provided that 'member states shall ensure the application of the principle that men and women shall receive equal pay for equal work'. Article 141 was amended by the Treaty of Amsterdam to refer to equal pay for work of equal value. Article 141 now reads ' 'Each member state shall ensure that the principle of equal pay for male and female workers for equal work or work of equal value is applied'. A definition of equal pay is also provided. Article 141 (2) defines pay as 'the ordinary or basic minimum wage or salary or any other consideration, whether in cash or in kind, which the worker receives directly or indirectly in respect of his employment from his employer. Article 141 (2) defines equal pay without discrimination to mean:

(a) that pay for the same work at piece rates shall be calculated on the basis of the same unit of measurement.; and

(b) that pay for the same work at time rates shall be the same for the same job.

The first significant Case under Article 141 concerned an applicant who was previously unsuccessful in challenging a discriminatory pension scheme based on national legislation and thus held to be outside of Community law competence. However, the claimant commenced a second action to challenge unequal pay. In Case 43/75 Defrenne v Sabena (No 2) a claim for compensation was made for the damage suffered from 1963 to February 1966 because Ms Defrenne was paid at a substantially lower rate than her male colleagues for the same work. Ms Defrenne was successful in her case. The Court of Justice held that the principle of equal pay was sufficiently clear and precise to have direct effects both vertically and horizontally. However, in response to the fears of employers that the Case would be retrospective if the judgement applied back to 1957, the Court of Justice declared that the ruling to be effective only from the date of the original litigation and any cases awaiting judgement.

The definition of pay

The term 'pay' has been progressively defined through case law. In Case 12/81 Garland v British Rail Engineering Article 119 (now 141) was held to include concessionary rail travel facilities for the family of an ex-employee. Pay, as interpreted by the Court of Justice also includes rules by which seniority/ loyalty payments are achieved in favour of full time employees.

In Case 184/89 Nimz v Hamburg, sick pay even though part of a statutory scheme, was seen as pay. In other cases a severance grant and compensation for lost wages for attendance on training courses were also seen as pay.

Pensions and pay

Directive 79/7 Article 7 stipulates that member states have the right to exclude from equal treatment the determination of pensionable age for the purposes of granting retirement pensions and old age pensions. However, several cases have highlighted the problems that arise between different member states and different laws and ways of thinking.

In Case C-262/88 Barber v Guardian Royal Exchange Assurance Group, Barber was made redundant by GRE at the age of 52. There was an agreed contracted-out pensions scheme. His redundancy package included a statutory redundancy payment, and an ex-gratia payment (top up) but entitlement to his occupational pension was deferred until the agreed pension age under the scheme of 62 for men and 57 for women. The agreement in the redundancy package was that if within ten years of the state pension ages, the pension could be obtained earlier. A redundant woman aged 52 would be entitled to immediate access to her pension as she was within ten years of the statutory pension age whereas Barber was not, which was the basis for the claim of unlawful discrimination. The defence claimed that there was a link to the pension age therefore the case fell under Directive 79/7 exemption, in which case it was unlawful discrimination.

The UK Government intervened and claimed that the scheme, which replaced the state scheme should be regarded as coming within social security and not within Article 199 (now 141). The Court of Justice concluded that the statutory redundancy pay and the benefits from his contracted out occupational pension scheme were 'pay' under Article 119. The deciding factor is whether the rules and thus payment of the specific scheme are part of the employment contract or by voluntary inclusion of the employer. Only if entirely to do with a compulsory state pension does a case fall outside Article 141. The Court of Justice emphasised the importance of the fact that the occupational pension scheme was funded without any contribution being made by the public authorities.

This particular case, the Barber case, gave rise to concerns as it was not expected that pensions should be treated as pay. It would mean that there was unlawful discrimination, which was not previously the case. The Court of Justice, following this case, announced that from the date of judgement of the Barber case, Article 141 would apply for all cases henceforth and not be retrospective. This would avoid huge sums in compensation being paid out.

Many other cases have arisen since the Barber case, seeking clearer definitions. In Case C-152/91 Neath v Hugh Steeper, it was held that inequality in employees contributions arising from actuarial factors such as life expectancy, which differed according to sex would not be caught by Article 141. The case involved the conversion of a periodic payment to a lump-sum payout. Whilst benefits and payments must be regarded as pay, this is not the case for contributions which determine the size of the fund, as other factors than a simple difference in sex are involved. The funding system to provide the amount of pension available does not come under Article 141.

Part-time work

The Part Time Worker Directive 97/81 has been problematic and thoroughly tested in the Court of Justice, and the concept of indirect discrimination which can be justified has developed.

Article 141 and Directive 75/117 clearly outlaw direct discrimination, on the grounds of gender. However, in Case 96/80 Jenkins v Kingsgate, the employers paid full time workers 10 per cent more per hour than part-time workers. This was, it was claimed, in order to discourage absenteeism and to achieve more efficient use of their machinery. All but one of the part-time workers were women. The Court of Justice held:

A difference in rates of remuneration between full and part time employees did not offend against Article 119 (now 141) provided that the difference was attributable to factors which were objectively justified and did not relate directly to discrimination based on sex.

and

If it is established that a considerably smaller percentage of women than men perform the number of hours necessary to be a full timer, the inequality will contravene Article 119 where, regard being had to the difficulties encountered by women in arranging to work the minimum number of hours per week, the pay policy of the undertaking cannot be explained by factors other than the discrimination based on sex.

The implication is that it is harder for women than men to work full-time because of commitments to family and home but this does not make it lawful to discriminate against them.

Objective justifications

In order to show that discrimination was objectively justified, the employer must show that the measures giving rise to the difference in treatment:

a) correspond to a genuine need of the enterprise
b) are suitable for attaining the objective pursued by the enterprise: and
c) are strictly necessary for that purpose, i.e. proportional.

Work of equal value

Work of equal value claims also causes difficulties because it is not often clear that two jobs are of the same value and an appraisal has to be carried out, either by a national court or a formal job appraisal scheme. Case C-127/92 Enderby v Frenchay Health Authority involved an equal value claim and the comparison of lower paid speech therapists (mainly women) with higher paid men pharmacists and clinical psychologists. The Court of Justice held that it was up to the national court to determine whether and to what extent the shortage of candidates for a job and the need to attract them by paying higher pay constituted an objectively justified ground for the difference in pay between jobs of equal value.

The Equal Treatment Directive

The Equal Treatment Directive 76/207 goes beyond the scope of Article 119 (now 141) which was concerned only with pay. The prohibition of discrimination on the grounds of sex was extended into many facets of employment relationships, including access, dismissal, appointment, retirement, training conditions and working conditions.

The protection of women regarding childbirth and maternity rights generally

Article 2 (7) of the Directive provides:

' This Directive shall be without prejudice to provisions concerning the protection of women, particularly as regards pregnancy and maternity'.

Directive Article 2(7) continues:

Women on maternity leave shall be entitled, after the end of her period of maternity leave, to return to her job or to an equivalent post on terms and conditions which are no less favourable to her and to benefit from any improvement in working conditions to which she would be entitled during her absence. Less favourable treatment of a woman related to pregnancy or maternity leave within the meaning of Directive 92/85/EEC shall constitute discrimination within the meaning of this directive.

Directive 92/85 concerns the protection of pregnant and breastfeeding workers. Article 10 in combination with Article 8 designates the period of special protection as from the beginning of pregnancy to the end of maternity leave (which must be a 14 week continuous period of leave) in which women are protected from dismissal for any reasons connected to pregnancy. After the period has expired the special protection is lost.

Dismissal during or after pregnancy

A series of cases has highlighted the effectiveness of the Community protection system. In C-421/92 Habermann-Beltermann v Arbeiterwohlfahrt, HB was employed on a permanent nights contract and was dismissed when discovered to be pregnant on the basis of a national law prohibiting the night time work of pregnant women. The employer argued that the prohibition of night work was allowed by the Directive and to that extent the Court of Justice agreed with the employer but not to justify dismissal. The Court of Justice held that neither national legislation nor employment contract rules could render void an employment contract by reason of the fact that the female worker was found to be pregnant. Dismissal was clearly disproportionate and the employer should have found alternative work within the company for her.

In Case C-32/93 Webb v EMO Air Cargo (UK) Ltd, a woman who was employed on an indefinite contract to replace her predecessor, who was on pregnancy and maternity leave, was dismissed when it was found she was also pregnant. The Court of Justice held this to be direct discrimination contrary to Articles 2(1) and 5(1) of the Directive 76/207.

Related secondary legislation
Occupational Pensions Directive 86/378

This directive extends the equal treatment principle to occupational as opposed to statutory pension schemes and applies similar rules to Directive 79/7.

The Self Employed Equal treatment Directive 86/613

This provides for the application of the equal treatment principle to the self-employed especially in respect of self-employed women during pregnancy and motherhood.

Parental Leave Directive 96/34

This Directive, which was enacted under the Social Policy Agreement and extended to the UK by Directive 97/75 applies the principle of equal treatment to the right to parental leave. It provides that all workers can obtain parental leave of three months to care for a new born or adopted child up to the age of 8 years. In seeking to claim leave and during leave itself workers are protected from dismissal.

Part-Time Workers Directive 97/81

This Directive was adopted under the Social policy Agreement and extended to the UK by Directive 98/23.Whilst not primarily aimed at addressing discrimination of women, the purpose of the directive, which is the removal of discrimination against part time workers, will have the ultimate effect of helping more women than men as more women are employed as part-timers.

Fixed-Term Workers Directive 99/70

First adopted under the social policy agreement, this Directive applied much of the same considerations about part-time work to fixed-term work which is defined in Clause 3 as a contract of employment where the end is predetermined by the completion of a period of time or task or event. Under this Directive, there should be no discrimination in comparison also with a full-time worker unless objectively justified.

****

Index

Emerald Publishing
www.emeraldpublishing.co.uk

106 Ladysmith Road
Brighton BN2 4EG

Other titles in the Emerald Series:

Law
Guide to Bankruptcy
Conducting Your Own Court case
Guide to Consumer law
Creating a Will
Guide to Family Law
Guide to Employment Law
Guide to European Union Law
Guide to Health and Safety Law
Guide to Criminal Law
Guide to Landlord and Tenant Law
Guide to the English Legal System
Guide to Housing Law
Guide to Marriage and Divorce
Guide to The Civil Partnerships Act
Guide to The Law of Contract
The Path to Justice
You and Your Legal Rights

Health
Guide to Combating Child Obesity
Asthma Begins at Home

Music
How to Survive and Succeed in the Music Industry

General
A Practical Guide to Obtaining probate

A Practical Guide to Residential Conveyancing
Writing The Perfect CV
Keeping Books and Accounts-A Small Business Guide
Business Start Up-A Guide for New Business
Finding Asperger Syndrome in the Family-A Book of Answers

For details of the above titles published by Emerald go to:

www.emeraldpublishing.co.uk